Character Education

Grades K–2

Teaching Values for Life

by
Kathleen Knoblock

Illustrated by
Renée C. Yates

Cover Design by
Annette Hollister-Papp

Publishers
Instructional Fair • TS Denison
Grand Rapids, Michigan 49544

CREDITS:

Author: Kathleen Knoblock
Illustrator: Renée C. Yates
Project Director: Sherrill B. Flora
Project Editor: Linda Wood
Copy Editor: Mandy Shear
Cover Design: Annette Hollister-Papp
Production: Linda T. Price
Photo Credit: Comstock, Inc.

ABOUT THE AUTHOR:

Kathleen Knoblock has been active in the education field for over 22 years, dividing her time equally between classroom teaching and product development for the instructional materials industry. Kathleen's approach to writing and designing educational products is to step into the mind of the user — child, teacher, or parent — to create activities that are practical, fun, and educationally sound.

Standard Book Number: 1-56822-480-X
Character Education: Teaching Values for Life (Gr. K–2)
SPCN: 990-219-4338

2400 Turner Avenue NW
Grand Rapids, Michigan 49544

Printed in the USA

Character Education

Today, to become productive citizens of the future, children need to do more than learn the three R's. They also need to develop a set of core values that they can call on throughout their lives to guide their attitudes and behavior. To meet this need, a nationwide movement has been implemented to strengthen individuals, families, and communities through character education.

Six "building blocks" of character — trustworthiness, respect, responsibility, fairness, caring, and citizenship — form the foundation of character education. Although addressed individually in this guide, these building blocks are inseparable parts of a complete attitude that can help children reduce risk behaviors, improve achievement, and develop overall integrity.

These goals cannot be accomplished through the efforts of any one teacher, parent, or institution. The responsibility for developing a nation of morally conscious students must be shared by all individuals and organizations — schools, families, churches, communities, and government. Only through shared commitment can we hope to raise the level of character consciousness.

This book offers a starting point. The activities in it are designed to help children learn to think critically so that they can evaluate their own decisions and attitudes. Further, these activities specifically reach out beyond the classroom — into students' families and communities — where much of the most important learning takes place.

Character education is not add-on curriculum. Rather, it is a method for accomplishing the existing goals of education — to help children develop *all* the skills they will need to become successful adults. Approach it as a subject that you can weave into your everyday interactions with children. Get started by integrating the teaching ideas, activities, and discussion cards into your regular curriculum. Soon you will see that the whole climate of your environment is becoming more positive. You may even find that guiding the development of character is the most rewarding part of your job as teacher or parent.

Features of This Guide

- Ideas, activities, and reproducible pages for each character trait
- Motivational cartoons and awards for each character trait
- Open-ended discussion cards for each character trait
- A bibliography of literature support (can be reproduced for parents)
- A letter to parents explaining the purpose of character education and suggesting ways they can help at home

Contents

*Reproducible

Trustworthiness • Respect • Responsibility • Fairness • Caring • Citizenship

Trustworthiness

The core of trust lies in expectations. We expect people to tell the truth, be honest, and keep their word. Those who meet our expectations are the ones who earn our trust.

In this unit, Trustworthy Tiger will help you help your children

- understand what it means to be trustworthy.
- begin to be able to make judgments about the trustworthiness of others.
- evaluate their own trustworthiness.

Individual Reflections

Who Can I Trust?

As adults, we want our children to be trustworthy and to value trustworthiness in others. We are not born distrusting others, yet the reality is that not everyone can be trusted. It is important that students know who they can trust. As they grow up, they must learn to balance their need to rely on others with their vulnerability to being hurt emotionally or physically.

It would be unwise to give young children the impression that they can trust everyone, yet it is vital for them to know and be able to identify certain people whom they can count on—people they can trust with their safety, their thoughts, and their feelings without fear of harm.

Begin by talking with your children about trust. Are all people honest? Can you expect every person you meet not to hurt you with words or actions? How can we tell which people to trust and which people not to trust? *A trustworthy person is someone you can be sure cares about you enough that he or she would not intentionally hurt you in any way.* After a thorough discussion, distribute photocopies of the activity on page 8. Then ask each child to identify one or more people he feels he can trust. If necessary, help the children record the names of these people.

Group Workout

Strategies for Teachers and Parents

Character education crosses boundaries between home, school, and community. Parents, teachers, and community members must all take responsibility for teaching and modeling the character traits we want to develop in our children. Here are some things you can do to help instill trustworthiness as a value that children will seek.

- Children learn by what they see and hear. Be aware of the behaviors you are modeling.
- Make your expectations clear. Expect honesty and truthfulness, and demonstrate those qualities yourself. Then let the child know that you trust him or her.
- Be on the lookout for opportunities to reinforce character building in your daily activities.
- Talk about trust. Be realistic, but avoid creating fearfulness of others.
- Point out situations in your everyday life in which you trust others—drivers, store clerks, signs, each other, and so on.
- Use stories and literature that teach lessons. For example, Grimm's fairy tale, "The Frog Prince," teaches the value of keeping one's word.

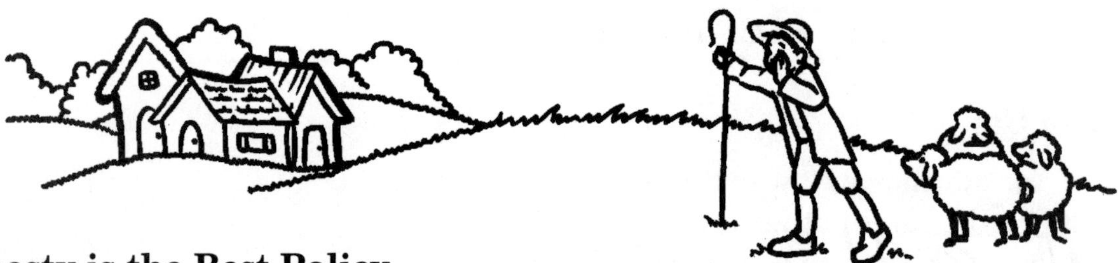

Honesty is the Best Policy

Tell or read the story of "The Boy Who Cried Wolf." Hold a discussion that encourages students to think about and respond to questions such as these:

1. Did the villagers start out trusting the boy? How do you know? (*Yes, because at first they believed him and came running to help.*)
2. Why didn't the villagers come to the boy's rescue when the wolf really did appear? (*They didn't believe him because he had lied to them before.*)
3. Why do you think the boy lied? (*He thought it was funny.*)
4. What happens when someone who is known to have lied tells the truth? (*People will not trust what he says.*)

The Boy Who Cried Wolf retold by Katherine Evans (Albert Whitman, 1960)
This is just one of several versions of the classic story.

Home-School Connections

1, 2, 3, You Can Count on Me!

Since behavior stems from internal values and individual choices, dictating from the outside is not the most effective way to instill values. For a value to become a part of a person's character, it must be internalized and the individual must take ownership of it.

The activity on page 9 asks students to take a pledge of trustworthiness and to add their personal commitment to it. Once children have done this, invite them to share their pledges with others at home. You may want to make extra copies of the activity for those whose families who wish to participate directly by filling out their own pledges.

Community Action

Role Playing

Give students opportunities to role-play situations that involve trust issues in and around the community. In each situation, discuss who is showing trustworthiness and why. Here are some ideas:

1. Two children are in the ice cream store. Together their cones cost $1.50. They give the clerk three one-dollar bills. She says that she only needs two.
2. A family is in a restaurant. They find a wallet lying on the seat. Dad takes it to the manager.
3. Some children are in the park. They see some older children spray-painting a park bench. They tell a police officer what they saw.
4. A neighbor borrows the lawn mower. Later, he brings it back.
5. Three children are invited to a surprise party for a friend. No one tells.

Name

Who Can I Trust?

Like you, Trustworthy Tiger sometimes has a problem or just needs to talk to someone. He knows that he cannot trust just anyone, so he thinks carefully about who he can trust. He knows it must be someone who cares about him and who would never try to hurt him.

Directions:
Think of one or more people you can trust to help you with a problem or to tell about your feelings. Write their names on Trustworthy Tiger's sign.

Name

1, 2, 3, You Can Count on Me!

Directions: Can others count on you to be trustworthy? If so, complete this pledge by promising to **tell the truth, be honest,** and **keep your word.**

You can count on me to . . .

1.

2.

3.

Trustworthy Tiger

DOES . . .

tell the truth.

DOESN'T . . .

cheat or lie.

Trustworthiness Award

You are now a member of Trustworthy Tiger's "I tell the truth" team.

Like me, Trustworthy Tiger, you can be counted on to tell the truth, be honest, and keep your word.

Respect

The foundation of respect is worth. Anything of value deserves a measure of respect. Foremost we must respect other people—their feelings, their beliefs, and their cultures. We must also respect other living things, including plants and animals, and the environment and natural resources that enable us to exist—the earth, the air, and the water. But respect extends much further. We respect others' physical space, property, and rights. We respect others' achievements, authority, and wisdom. And, we respect our country and the various social organizations to which we belong.

In this unit, Respectful Rabbit will help you help your children

- understand that respect means treating others as you would like to be treated.
- learn that good manners are a way to show respect.
- recognize behavior as respectful or disrespectful.

Group Workout

Different Yet the Same

Ask your librarian for a copy of W. Nikola-Lisa's book *Bein' With You This Way*. This beautifully illustrated book celebrates cultural diversity through the story of a group of children at play who discover that although they all look different, they are really just the same. The text has a rhythm that flows like a song punctuated with repeating refrains like "Ah-ha" and "Oh yeah!" Read the story twice and your students are likely to "sing" along. Follow up with a discussion of how, like the children in the story, they are different yet the same.

Bein' With You This Way by W. Nikola-Lisa (Lee & Low, 1994)
From a child's-eye view, discovering physical differences only adds to the joy of playing and being together.

Individual Reflections

Would You Like It?

Respect is an act of selflessness—placing concern for others equal to or above concern for oneself. This is a difficult concept for young children to grasp because they have not yet fully developed the ability to step outside themselves to view things from other perspectives. Rather than asking a child to imagine how someone *else* feels under certain circumstances, you may have more success asking her how *she* would feel under those circumstances. Use any or all of the following hypothetical situations to explore issues of respect.

Would you like it if someone . . .

- called you a name?
- pushed you out of line?
- broke your favorite toy?
- laughed when you made a mistake?
- teased you?
- blamed you for something you didn't do?
- took your share of something?

After discussing the feelings elicited by these actions, tell the children that Respectful Rabbit has a special rule that people can follow to avoid hurting each other's feelings. The rule is very simple: *Treat others as you would like to be treated.*

Give each child a copy of the reproducible on page 14. Read each statement and ask the child to decide whether Respectful Rabbit would or would not do each thing described.

Home-School Connections

A Matter of Manners

Manners are an important part of showing respect and concern for the rights and feelings of others. Let Respectful Rabbit remind children that saying *Please, Thank you, Excuse me,* and *I'm Sorry* shows respect for others. After completing page 15, invite students to join the "Manners Matter Team" at school and at home. As part of the team, their job is to "catch" classmates and family members using good manners and to thank them for being considerate.

Community Action

My World, My Community

In addition to respecting people, we want our children to respect the environment and all of its inhabitants. To young children, the "world" consists of their immediate surroundings. To help your students develop respect for the earth and its resources, begin in your own backyard.

Take the group outside onto school grounds. Ask them to look around them and talk about what they see—grass? trees? birds? trash? anything broken? writing on the walls? and so on. Discuss the word *environment.* Ask students why they think it is important to respect the environment and what they can do to show their respect.

Finally, arrange a walking field trip around your community. Invite each child to bring along a bag in which to collect trash. (Be sure to tell them ahead of time what kinds of things not to pick up—broken glass, garbage, and so on.)

Upon your return, have children draw pictures about what they did on the field trip and write (or dictate) sentences about what they learned from the experience.

Name ______________________________

What Would She Do?

Directions: Respectful Rabbit cares about the feelings of others. Decide if she would or would not do each thing. Put a ✓ in the right column.

	would	would not
Pay back money she borrowed.		
Call someone a name.		
Make noises at the table.		
Replace something she lost or broke.		
Blame her sister for something she did.		
Take the biggest piece of cake.		
Throw trash on the floor.		
Send her Grandpa a birthday card.		
Say she didn't like a gift she got.		
Ask her friend to lie about something.		
Take a pencil from someone's desk.		
Cut in line.		
Help out at home.		
Do her chores without being asked.		
Throw a rock at an animal.		
Give a phone message she took.		
Tell someone to "Get Lost."		
Tease and scare her little brother.		
Bother the dog when he is asleep.		

Name ________________________________

Manners Matter

Directions: Respectful Rabbit knows the importance of good manners. Write what she would say in each situation.

• Please **• Thank you** **• Excuse me** **• I'm sorry**

Respectful Rabbit got a gift from Grandma.

Respectful Rabbit wanted another fresh juicy carrot.

Respectful Rabbit sneezed very loudly.

Respectful Rabbit accidentally stepped on her brother's paw.

Respectful Rabbit

DOES . . .

treat everything the way she would like to be treated.

DOESN'T . . .

do anything that would hurt anyone or damage anything.

Congratulations! You have earned Respectful Rabbit's

Respectfulness Award

Like me, Respectful Rabbit, you treat others the way you would want to be treated.

Responsibility

Adults sometimes feel overwhelmed by life's many pressures and responsibilities. A young child does not carry such burdens. A child's concerns are for himself and generally are limited to the here and now. But, that is where the seeds of responsibility are planted. The first steps toward growth occur when a child begins to take responsibility for himself. This even a young child can do.

In this unit, Responsible Rhino will help you help your children

- begin to take a share of responsibility for their own personal care and safety.
- learn that they have responsibilities as members of groups — school, family, and community.
- recognize excuses as a method of shirking responsibility.

Individual Reflections

It's My Job

To a young child, the world seems to revolve around her. Before we can expect a child to take on responsibility for others, we must first see that she develops a sense of responsibility for her own well-being. If you ask a young child, "Do you have a job?" you might hear a giggle and an "of course not!" But you can easily get the child to admit that she actually has several "jobs" — to go to school and learn, to keep herself clean, to take care of her things.

Let each child think about the things she does to take responsibility for herself — brushing her own teeth, bathing, getting dressed, going to school on time, listening in class, doing her homework, keeping her room neat, and so on. Make a list of these "responsibilities" on a chart. Then give each child a sheet of drawing paper and crayons. At the top, have her copy (or write for her) *It's my job to. . . .* Then tell her to draw a picture of herself carrying out one of her responsibilities. Children who can write can complete the sentence with a phrase from the chart. Very young children can simply draw the picture and explain what they are doing in it.

Group Workout

Me, Myself, and Us

It is important early on to help children realize that they are not only individuals but also members of many groups—friends, class, their family, the community. For there to be cooperation within a group, every member must feel that he is part of the group and that he has a stake in it. Here's a fun way to promote individual responsibility within a group.

Choose a stuffed animal to be your class mascot. First, let the group give the mascot a name. (You can take suggestions and vote.) Next, tell children that "Marvin the Monkey" needs to be carefully watched and taken care of. It will be everyone's responsibility to make sure that he is. Marvin cannot be left alone! Someone has to take Marvin to lunch, out to recess, and even home for the night. At this point, you will have enthusiastic volunteers asking for the job!

Tell students that every member of the class is expected to take a turn being totally responsible for Marvin for an entire day. That person must not only take Marvin everywhere with him at school, but also take him home at night and bring him back again the next morning. Use a calendar or sign up sheet to assign each child a day. If there is continued interest after everyone has had one turn, repeat the schedule.

Who Will Help?

Go out of your way to make every child feel that he or she is an important part of the group. (This is especially critical in families in which the child is the "baby.") Explain that everyone in the group has jobs to do and is expected to "pitch in." Here are two suggestions for helping children take responsibility.

- Read the story "The Little Red Hen." In it, the Red Hen asks the farm animals, "Who will help me make the bread?" Each animal responds, "Not I." So the Red Hen does it all herself. Only when it is time to eat the bread are the others willing to help! Discuss the story and talk about how sharing the responsibility allows everyone to share in the benefits as well.
- Acknowledge a child when he or she takes responsibility, especially without having to be prompted. Example: "I see you cleaned up without my having to remind you. Thank you for being so responsible."

Home-School Connections

Excuses, Excuses

As part of their families, many children have specific responsibilities at home. Help your students see the importance of both accepting responsibility and following through with it. Give each child a copy of pages 20 and 21. Talk about Responsible Rhino. Then introduce "The Excuses"—animal characters that have familiar reasons for not fulfilling responsibilities: "Responsible Rhino," "Too Tired Turtle," "I'm-Busy Beaver," "Forgetful Ferret," and "Later Llama." Let children color and cut out the characters. Then have them spread them out on their desks.

Tell children that you will be making statements that might be made at home or at school. Instruct them to hold up the character you mention and answer aloud as the character would. Then repeat the statement. This time, instruct children to answer as Responsible Rhino would. Finally, repeat the statement a third time, and have children write out their answers on their worksheets (page 21). (Write on the board any words students might need to have spelled for them.)

Children will easily learn the names of "The Excuses." Extend the value of this activity by letting the characters become part of your strategy for dealing with everyday situations in the classroom. For example, when it is clean-up time, remind students that Too Tired Turtle is not in their class.

Community Action

Community Helpers

The social studies curriculum for primary students typically includes a look at community helpers. First, discuss how police officers, firefighters, teachers, nurses, doctors, and other community helpers take responsibility for others in the community.

Next, divide the class into groups of four or five students. Assign each group one kind of community helper. Provide large sheets of butcher paper, markers, and scissors. Ask groups to trace one child's outline on the paper, cut it out, and work together to decorate it as their community helper. Finally, have students label their community helper and briefly describe his or her main responsibility in the community. Post the models on a large wall in or outside your classroom.

Name ______________________

Responsible Rhino Vs. The Excuses

Directions: Color and cut out this cast of characters. Use them for the activity your teacher will explain.

Name ______________________________

Excuses, Excuses

Directions: Read what each character said.
Then write what you would say.

Mother: Did you brush your teeth?

Forgetful Ferret: I forgot.

Responsible Rhino: Yes!

You: ______________________________

Teacher: If you're done, please put away the toys.

Too Tired Turtle: I'm too tired.

Responsible Rhino: OK. I'll do it now.

You: ______________________________

Friend: Will you help me find my book?

I'm Busy Beaver: Ask someone else. I'm busy.

Responsible Rhino: Sure. I'll help.

You: ______________________________

Father: Please take out the trash.

Later Llama: Later. I don't feel like it now.

Responsible Rhino: I'll be right there.

You: ______________________________

Responsible Rhino

DOES . . .

the jobs he is expected to do and helps others when he can.

DOESN'T . . .

expect someone else to take care of things he should do himself.

Responsibility Club Membership

As a member of Responsible Rhino's Responsibility Club, you do the jobs you are expected to do and you help others when you can.

Fairness

When you hear the words "It's not fair!" coming from a child, it probably means that the child has failed to get something that he believes he deserved. A child's beliefs about what he should get are based on his expectations, which stem from previous experiences, promises, and comparisons of himself with others. You can help children develop a realistic sense of fairness by being consistent, by making sure that expectations are clear, and by helping him understand that certain rights come only with age or achievement.

In this unit, Fair Fox will help you help your children

- distinguish between intentional and unintentional actions.
- learn to take turns when speaking and to listen to others.
- recognize an inequality as fair or unfair.

Individual Reflections

An Important Distinction

Children are very quick to point out anything that they perceive to be unfair. Although they are keenly aware of when their rights have been violated, they often misinterpret a key component of fairness—intent. An accidental event can easily be perceived as a intentional act.

Children tend to react rather than reflect. Use the activity on page 26 to help your children think more carefully about fairness. Read each statement aloud. Ask the children to decide if it describes a situation that is fair or one that is unfair. After everyone has finished, talk about the results. Guide children to conclude that an action may be viewed quite differently depending on whether it was an accident or whether it was intentional.

Group Workout

What Is a Fair Share?

Divide the class into groups of four. Give each group a copy of the activity on page 27 and a bag containing 25 dried beans. Tell students to imagine that they are baby foxes and that the beans are fox "food." Instruct them to divide up the beans so that each baby fox gets the same amount. Discuss the results.

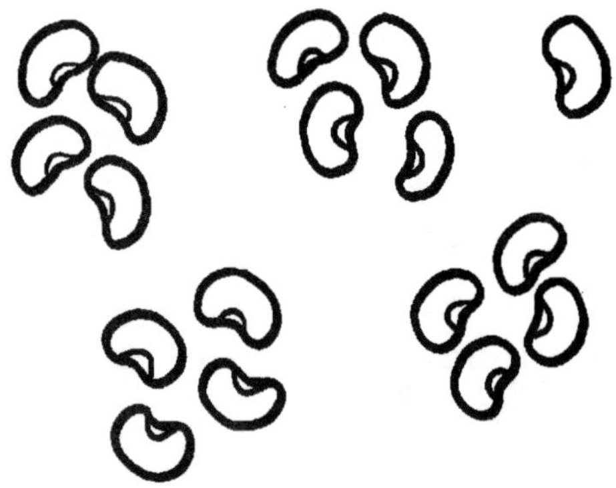

Now appoint one member of the group to be Mother Fox. Again tell groups that they are to divide the beans *fairly*. Observe them carefully to see if different groups go about solving the problem differently. Did any group give more beans to the mother because she was bigger and "needed" more food? Conclude by asking students if fair always means equal.

One at a Time, Please!

Even very young children have a distinct sense of fairness. In fact, most children will quickly protest any situation in which they feel they have been treated unfairly (valid or not). They are quick to blame others and can be quite vocal in expressing their views. Arguments invariably flare up, and everyone involved is anxious to tell his or her "side" of the story. It can be frustrating to try to sort out the facts with everyone talking at once!

Try this approach to give each person a fair chance to have his say. Choose an object, such as a beanbag, foam ball, or your stuffed animal mascot (see page 18). Whenever a disagreement erupts, have everyone sit in a circle with their hands folded in their laps. Explain that you are going to hand the object to one person at a time. While that person has the object, she, and only she, can speak. No one may interrupt. She will have two minutes (or whatever time limit you set) to say everything she wants to say. Then you will pass the object to another person. Only after everyone has had a fair chance to speak will you attempt to resolve the problem.

Extend this idea throughout your everyday activities to reinforce taking turns when speaking. For example, hold the mascot yourself when you are speaking. When you ask a question during a lesson, hand the mascot to a student. That person then knows that she "has the floor"—it is her turn to speak and everyone else is to be listening. This is an excellent way to encourage reluctant children to speak, too. Simply hand the mascot to a student as a signal that you want her to respond. For the very shy, just having something in her hand as she speaks may help.

Home-School Connections

More or Less

A major fairness issue that concerns young children arises when the child feels that he is not receiving the same treatment as someone else. It may in fact be true that the child is being treated differently than another child, but this does not automatically mean that the treatment is unfair. Children often question inequities because they don't understand why they exist. And it is difficult for them to assess what they "deserve" without a reasonable and adequate explanation. For example, if a six-year-old has a bedtime of 8:00 p.m., it is difficult for him to understand why his ten-year-old sister is allowed to stay up later.

Read aloud to students Judith Viorst's book *Alexander, Who Used to Be Rich Last Sunday.* In this story, three brothers receive a dollar each from their grandparents. The youngest, Alexander, spends his dollar and then claims that it is unfair that his brothers still have money and he doesn't.

After you have shared the story, let students discuss why Alexander feels that this situation is unfair. Ask them if they agree with Alexander, and why or why not. Challenge students to explain whose responsibility it is that Alexander has less money than his brothers

Finally, encourage students to talk about times when they may have felt like Alexander. If you think your students are mature enough, hold a discussion about allowances: Should allowances be given for chores, given for no reason, not given at all? Should older children get bigger allowances than younger children?

Alexander, Who Used to Be Rich Last Sunday by Judith Viorst (Atheneum, 1978)

Ms. Viorst has a gift for portraying the everyday experiences and unique feelings of young children in a humorous and touching way.

You may want to share these titles as well: *Alexander and the Terrible, Horrible, No Good, Very Bad Day* and *My Mama Says There Aren't Any Zombies, Ghosts, Vampires, Creatures, Demons, Monsters, Fiends, Goblins, or Things.*

Name ______________________________

Upset!

Directions: Decide if it would be fair to be upset in each situation. Circle **yes** or **no**. Be prepared to tell why.

Bobby stepped on Rico's shoelace and Rico tripped. Would it be fair for Rico to be upset with Bobby?

Yes **No**

Sara called Yuri stupid when he didn't make the goal during a soccer game. Would it be fair for Yuri to be upset with Sara?

Yes **No**

When Dee got home from school, she found her baby sister playing with Dee's favorite doll. Would it be fair for Dee to be upset with her baby sister?

Yes **No**

Jan promised to call Marlee on Saturday, but she never called. Would it be fair for Marlee to be upset with Jan?

Yes **No**

Name ______________________________

Fair Share

Directions: Use your bag of "food" to solve each problem. Draw the number of "food" pieces that each fox gets.

1. Divide the food among the foxes so that each has an *equal share*.

Fox 1 	**Fox 2** 	**Fox 3** 	**Fox 4** 

Are there any leftovers? ____________

2. Now divide the food so that each fox has a *fair share*.

Mother 	**Baby 1** 	**Baby 2** 	**Baby 3** 

Are there any leftovers? ____________

Fair Fox

DOES . . .

take turns, share, and consider others.

DOESN'T . . .

interrupt or take more than her share.

"Fairness First" Team

Welcome to Fair Fox's "Fairness First" team! We take turns, share, and consider others.

Caring

Kindness, compassion, understanding, sharing, helping—these are all aspects of caring. Perhaps of all the character traits, caring is the one comes most naturally to young children. The warmth of receiving and giving care is a feeling we all naturally seek, and children readily feel empathy for others. The opposing forces—cruelty, greed, and insensitivity—are learned. Being able to give to another, whether it is a parent, a friend, or a bug on the sidewalk, allows even the youngest child to feel powerful, needed, and appreciated.

In this unit, Caring Koala will help you help your children

- learn to give compliments.
- appreciate ways people help and care for one another.
- show compassion for others.

Group Workout

"I Like You" Charts

Giving compliments is an easy way for people to show that they care. This self-esteem-building activity gives your children a chance to practice pointing out postive things about each other. It is also a great way to close out each day.

I like Michelle because she always shares. (Danny)

I like Michelle because she is my friend. (Karla)

I like Michelle because she let me borrow a pencil. (Ann)

I like Michelle because she helped me once. (Tuwanda)

I like Michelle because she is nice to me. (Randy)

At the beginning of the day, draw a child's name at random. Tell students that throughout the day, they are to bc thinking of things that they like about that person. At the end of the day, gather the group in front of a chart. Write: *I like* ___________ *because* ___________. (Fill in the child's name.) Ask students to tell you how to complete the sentence. When you use someone's suggestion, ask him to sign his name after it on the chart. Repeat this activity until you have at least five complete sentences about that child. Roll up the chart, tie it with a yarn bow, and give it to the child.

Individual Reflections

You Suit Me to a Tee

This activity encourages each child to reflect on what he or she cares about and to share it with others. Give each child a copy of page 32. Instruct children to fill in their names at the top of the tee. Then have them think about the things they care about. If necessary, make a chart of suggestions—family, pets, friends, books, the earth, and so on. Ask the children to complete the sentence, then decorate the tee as if it were a real shirt they could wear.

Label a bulletin board "You Suit Me to a Tee." String a piece of yarn across it like a clothesline. Have each child cut out his or her tee and attach it to the clothesline with real clothespins.

Home-School Connections

Touched by Koko

If there is one story that touches the hearts of almost everyone who reads it, it is *Koko's Kitten* by Dr. Francine Patterson. This is the true account of a psychologist's work with a gorilla named Koko, who not only learned sign language but who also was able to express a wide range of emotions. Children will be fascinated by the photographs of Koko caring for her tiny pet kitten—caressing, tickling, feeding, and grooming it. The text is written in clear, simple language. Even the youngest child will hang on every word.

After sharing the story, talk with children about what it means to care. Discuss how Koko cared for her kitten as if it were her own baby. Talk about how families care for each other. If your children are not yet reading and writing, invite them to draw a picture of Koko and her kitten or to reenact a scene from the story with stuffed animals. Older children can fold a sheet of drawing paper in fourths and draw in each section a different way their families care for them. Have them label each drawing with a sentence or phrase.

Koko's Kitten by Francine Patterson (Scholastic, 1985)

Children and adults alike will be fascinated by this real-life tale. They can learn more about Koko in Dr. Patterson's companion book, *The Story of Koko.*

Community Action

Make Someone Smile

This activity will help your children learn that caring reaches beyond friends and family into the community. Contact a hospital or convalescent home for the names of people who would like to receive letters from your students. If there is no hospital or home nearby, perhaps you know of someone who lives alone who would appreciate your students' good wishes.

Share with students Arnold Lobel's book *Frog and Toad Are Friends*. Talk about how Frog and Toad show they care by cheering each other up when they are sad or lonely. Tell children that even though they are young, they have the power to make someone smile! After reading the story "The Letter," explain to students that sometimes people have no one like Frog to cheer them up when they are sad and lonely. Ask students if they would like to cheer up someone who has no family, is in the hospital, or lives in a convalescent home. Then invite them to use the pattern on page 33 to make a cheerful greeting for someone on your list. Collect and deliver the cards. If possible, take your children along!

Frog and Toad Are Friends by Arnold Lobel (HarperCollins, 1970)

The adventures of two friends are told with sensitivity and humor.

Trustworthiness • Respect • Responsibility • Fairness • **Caring** • Citizenship

Name ______________________

You Suit Me to a Tee

Directions: Design a tee-shirt that shows something you care about. Write your name at the top of the tee. Complete the sentence. Decorate and cut out the tee. Then hang it up to share what you care about with others.

Name ______________________________

Cheer Up!

Directions: Color and cut out Caring Koala and her sign. Paste it on the front of a half-sheet of construction paper folded down to make a card. On the inside of the card write one of these messages, or make up your own.

I'm thinking of you.
You are special.
Someone cares.

Caring Koala

DOES . . .

share, show kindness, and is thoughtful.

DOESN'T . . .

act mean, selfish, or thoughtless.

The "I" Care" Clan

You are a member of Caring Koala's "I Care" clan! We share and we are kind and thoughtful toward others.

Citizenship

Teach children that they are citizens of many groups — their class, their family, their community, and their country. Every citizen has a responsibility to follow the rules, obey the laws, respect authority, contribute to the group, protect the environment, and conserve resources.

In this unit, Good Citizen Goose will help you help your children

- recognize that they are citizens of many groups.
- understand that citizenship involves group commitment.
- become more familiar with their neighborhood community.

Individual Reflections

Citizenship in the Classroom

Begin this activity with a little story: Once there was a boy who lived all alone on a hill. He didn't have anything to be concerned about except himself. He didn't have to obey any rules, or even clean up after himself. But even though the boy could do whatever he pleased, he was not happy. He needed other people. One day a hunter found the boy sitting in a pile of trash he had created. He was crying. "What a mess," said the hunter. "Are you alone here?" The boy nodded and said, "May I come live in the village with you?" The hunter thought for a moment. "Yes. You are welcome to come live with the others. But you will have to learn to follow some rules and care about others." "OK," said the boy, and the hunter took the boy into the village and introduced him as a new citizen.

Ask children if they would rather live alone and do anything they want or live with others and follow rules. Talk about what it means to be a citizen of a group — community, country, family, or classroom.

People tend to care more about people they know than people they don't know. Promote group cohesion in your class by helping children get to know one another. Ask each child to invite the class to get to know him or her better. One at a time have children tell the group about themselves, where they live, what they like, and so on. Make a chart of prompt questions for children to refer to as they talk, or prompt children by using an interview format.

Group Workout

Using the Telephone

Talking on the telephone is often the first or only means of communication a person has with other people. As a citizen of their family, every child should learn to use the telephone properly and safely.

First, each child should understand that when answering the telephone at home, he or she represents the family. Talk about etiquette and safety when answering the phone. For example, after politely saying "Hello," the child should always ask the person calling to identify himself, who he is calling for, and the purpose of his call. Ask students what they should do or say if someone should ask them if they are alone? if someone refuses to identify himself? if someone says she is selling something? if someone says rude things?

Next, talk about using the phone to call others. Discuss questions such as these: How should you ask for the person you are calling? What if you reach an answering machine? How would you call your parent at work? Who would you call if there was an emergency, such as a fire?

Ask for volunteers to role-play different kinds of calls with you:

- You are calling their home to ask for a parent.
- They are calling your home to ask for a friend and they reach a machine.
- You are a receptionist at their parent's place of work when they call.
- You call their home and ask if they are alone.

Let students role-play different types of telephone calls. If possible, let them use real (disconnected) or play phones. Follow up this activity with the activity under "Community Action" on the following page.

Home-School Connections

Citizenship at School and at Home

Explain to students that part of the responsibility of being a citizen involves following rules and doing their part to ensure their own safety and that of others. No matter what kind of group a person belongs to, there are almost always rules designed to protect the rights of its members and to keep them from harm.

As citizens of the school, your students are expected to follow the rules. Brainstorm with the class a list of rules you have at school—in the classroom, at the library, in the lunchroom, on the playground, in the bathrooms, and during fire drills. As students mention each rule, ask them why they think that rule is needed. For example, "No running in the halls" is to protect their safety.

Next, ask the children to think about the rules they have at home. Remind them that every family is unique and that the rules may vary from one home to the next. As they mention each rule, record it on a chart. Ask students to explain why that rule is important in their household.

Give each child a copy of page 38, "House Rules." Instruct students to write their names (and addresses if possible) on the roof of the house, then draw pictures of themselves and members of their family looking out of the windows. Have younger students choose a house rule from the chart to copy in the center of the house. Older children can write several rules on a separate sheet of lined paper, cut apart the top and bottom half of the house, and attach it to the top and bottom of their page. If you wish, have students display their house rules on a bulletin board titled "Citizenship at Home."

Community Action

Everyone's in the Book

Ask children if they know of a book in which they can find the names and addresses of people and places in their community. If they can't guess, show them a local telephone book. Talk about the different sections of the book—emergency information, the white pages, and the yellow pages.

Page 39 is designed as a family project to be completed at home. Explain that the project is a kind of scavenger hunt in the telephone book. Tell them that as they work with a family member to find information in the telephone book, they will be learning more about who and what is in their community.

Give each child a copy of the page. Instruct children to fill out as much of it as they can by themselves and to enlist the help of a family member to complete the rest. Allow plenty of time for students and their families to work on the page.

Name

House Rules

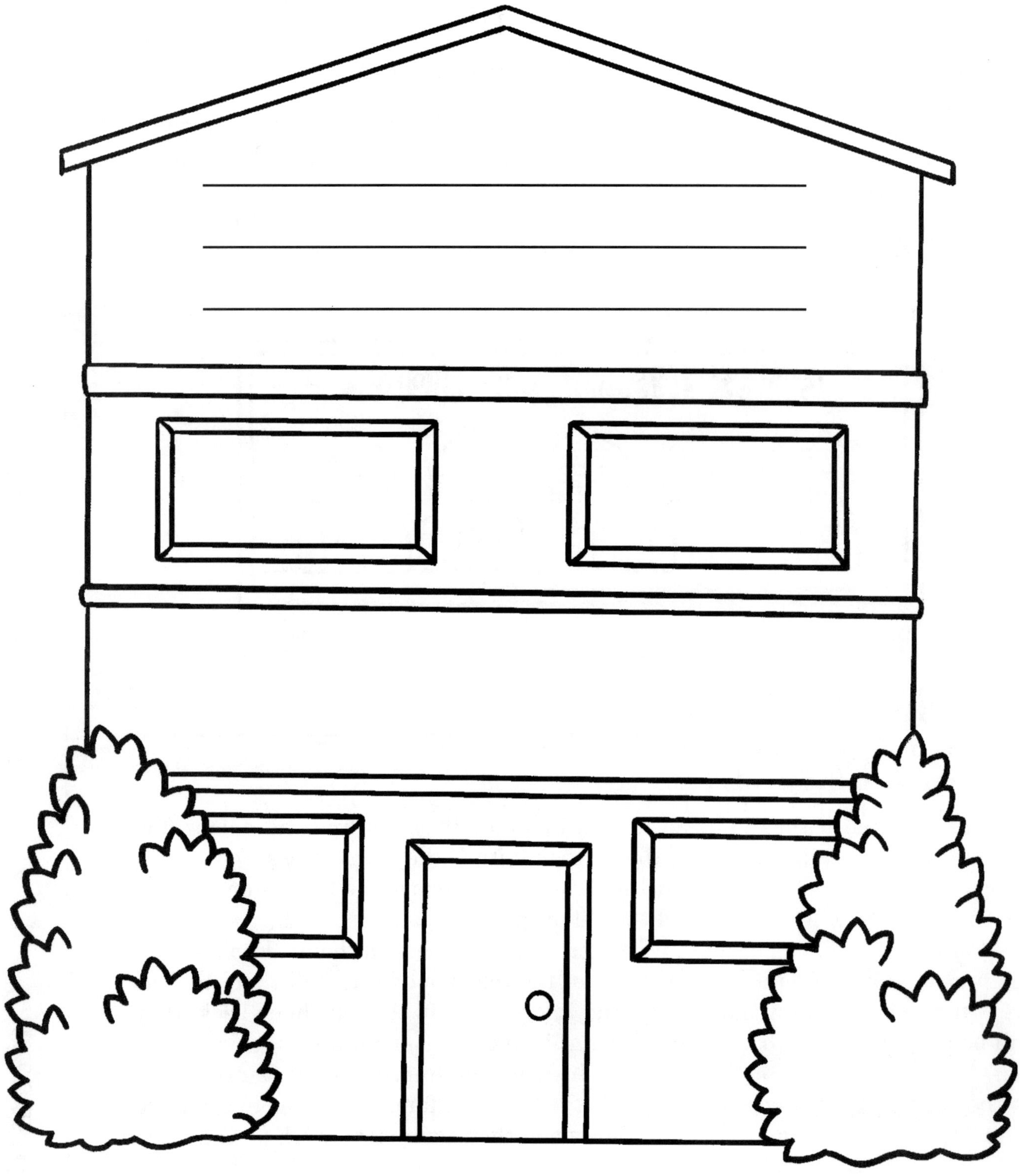

Name ______________________________

Community Search

Directions: Work with a family member to complete this information page about your community. You will need a telephone book to help you.

1. The name of my community is ______________________.
2. The name of my street is __________________________.
3. ____________________ is the name of a grocery store in my community. It is on ____________________ street.
4. In an emergency I could reach the police by dialing __________.
5. To find the name of a restaurant in my community, I could look in the ____________ pages of the phone book.
6. Find the phone number of your school. __________________
7. The name of a bank in my community is _______________.
8. Where in the community could you go to buy a pet? __________ ____
9. Where is the nearest post office? ____________________ ____
10. One of my neighbor's names is ______________________. Their phone number is __________________________.
11. If needed help I could call ____________________________ at ____________________________.

Good Citizen Goose

DOES . . .

**follow the rules
take responsibility,
and is careful.**

DOESN'T . . .

**break the rules, do
less than her share,
or be careless.**

Citizenship Award

Like Good Citizen Goose, you follow the rules, do your share, and are careful.

Discussion Cards—*Trustworthiness*

But She Wouldn't Mind . . .

Trustworthy Tiger was getting ready to go out the door to school. Suddenly he remembered that he needed a dollar for lunch at school. He spotted his mom's purse on the table. Mom was getting dressed for work. He didn't want to bother her, and besides he was late already.

Would Trustworthy Tiger go into Mom's purse and take the dollar he needed?

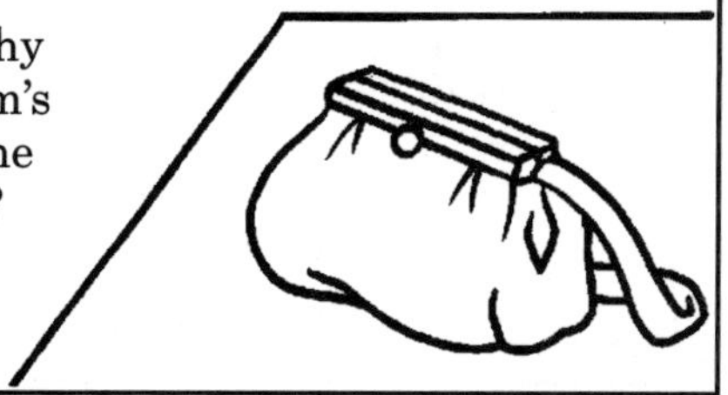

Just This Once . . .

Trustworthy Tiger did his spelling assignment as usual. And, as usual, Bully Bull didn't. On the way to school Bully Bull asked Trustworthy Tiger if he could copy his answers—just this once.

Would Trustworthy Tiger let Bully Bull have his answers?

Uh, Oh!

Trustworthy Tiger was playing ball in the house. He was being careful but the ball slipped out of his paws, bounced on the floor, and knocked over a lamp. He knew he shouldn't have been playing ball in the house. The lamp was ok, but the bulb was broken. His parents wouldn't notice until they went to turn on the light.

Would Trustworthy Tiger wait until his parents asked about the broken light, then tell them that he didn't know how it got broken?

I'll Get Around to It . . .

Trustworthy Tiger promised to take out the trash right after school. But when he got home, there was a show on television he wanted to watch.

Would Trustworthy Tiger break his word and watch the show instead of taking out the trash as he promised?

Discussion Cards—*Respect*

Because It's Fun

Goofy Gopher thinks it's fun to pick on bunnies. Sometimes he chases them into their holes. Sometimes he calls them "Big Ears." When they start to cry, he just laughs and scampers away.

What can the little bunnies do?

Someone Else Will Do It

You can always tell when Messy Mouse has been eating. There are paper wrappers and chewed up bits of food wherever she's been. Messy Mouse thinks someone else will clean up after her. The other mice are tired of cleaning up after Messy Mouse so they can have a nice place to eat.

What can the other mice do?

Discussion Cards—*Respect* continued

Who Cares?

Mother Squirrel was not feeling well. She decided to lie down and rest for a while. Squeaky Squirrel and Whiney Squirrel began to run around making all kinds of racket. Squeaky started to scream when he lost the game. Whiney Squirrel woke Mother Squirrel up to ask her to make her a walnut pie.

What can Mrs. Squirrel do?

You Took It

Blaming Bear started the day with three new pencils. At the end of the day, she only had two. "Someone stole my pencil," she thought. "Jerry Bear has a pencil. It's probably mine!" So she grabbed the pencil out of Jerry Bear's hand. "You took my pencil!" Blaming Bear shouted at Jerry Bear.

What can Jerry Bear do?

Discussion Cards—*Responsibility*

But *I* Didn't Drop Them There

When Responsible Rhino was going to get a drink at the water fountain, he spotted a pair of scissors on the floor. Even though he didn't drop them there, Responsible Rhino decided to pick them up and put them where they belong. Why would he do that?

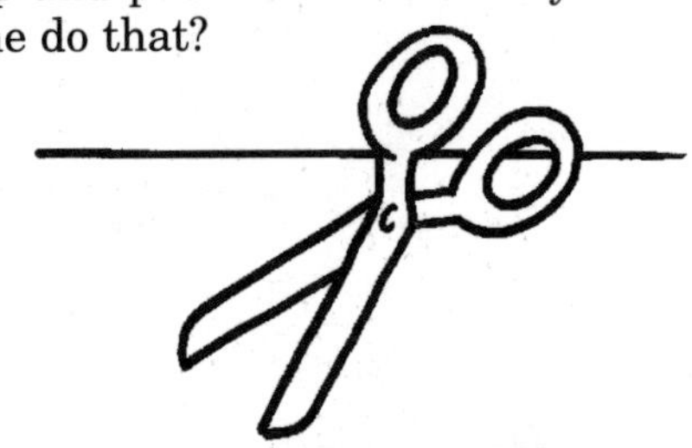

Lost and Not Found

Responsible Rhino had a book borrowed from the library. The day it was due back, he couldn't find the book. He went to the librarian and told her. She said if it wasn't found, he would have to pay for it. After a week, the book still hadn't turned up. Responsible Rhino was saving for a game he wanted, but he took the money from his bank and paid for the book. Why did he do that?

Finders Keepers

Responsible Rhino was at the grocery store helping his mother shop for food. While he was getting cans of soup from the shelf he found a wallet that someone must have put down and forgot to pick up. He looked inside. There was a name, some cards, and $20. He could have taken the money and left the wallet there. He could have taken the money and turned in the wallet. But Responsible Rhino turned in the wallet *and* the money. Why would he do that?

No Excuse

Responsible Rhino's club needed to raise money for a project they wanted to do. When the club leader asked for volunteers to help by donating old clothes and toys for a sale, some answers she got were, "I'm too busy" and "I can't." Then Responsible Rhino said, "I'll look for some things tonight." He was the one who didn't make an excuse. Even if he didn't feel like helping, he thought it was important to try. Why?

Discussion Cards—*Fairness*

But I Want One, Too!

It was Micky Monkey's twelfth birthday and he got a brand new bike. Millie Monkey, his little sister, made a scene when she saw the new bike. "I want one, too!" she cried.

Is it fair for Millie to think she should have a new bike, too? Why or why not?

He Shouldn't Get Away

Yesterday Mom baked a dozen cookies. Before Albert Aardvark had even one, his brother Allen and his friends ate them all! Today, Mom baked a dozen more. Albert said Allen shouldn't get any.

Should Allen get any of the cookies? Why or why not? What is a fair solution to the problem?

TV Squawking

Sometimes the Parrot family squabbles over television time. Polly wants to watch one thing and Peter wants to watch another. Peter says that because Polly is younger, what she wants shouldn't matter.

Is it fair for Peter to think that? Should Perry get to watch what he wants just because he is older? What is a fair solution to the problem?

More Important

Freddie Frog and his buddy Frank had been planning a special day for weeks. The day before they were to go, Frank called. "I'm sorry. I can't go," said Frank. "My Grandma's very sick and my whole family is going to see her." Freddie scowled and said, "Who cares about your Grandma? This is more important."

Was it fair for Freddie to be mad at Frank? Why or why not?

Discussion Cards—*Caring*

I Can Help

Caring Koala was on his way out to play when he heard crying coming from his baby sister's room. He went to see what was the matter. She was sitting on the floor trying to tie her own shoes.

What are some things Caring Koala could do to help his sister feel better?

The New Kid

One day at school a new student joined Caring Koala's class. He looked a little lost and scared.

What are some things Caring Koala could do to help the new student feel welcome?

Discussion Cards—*Caring* continued

The Birthday Party

For Caring Koala's birthday, his mom said he could invite five friends to a party. Caring Koala had more than five friends.

What are some ways Caring Koala could decide who to invite and how to avoid hurting anyone's feelings?

How About a Hug?

When Caring Koala's friend came to school one day, he looked very sad. When Caring Koala asked why he looked so sad, his friend told him that his dog had died.

What are some things Caring Koala could do or say to show his friend he cared?

Discussion Cards—*Citizenship*

Up for Grabs

Good Citizen Goose was waddling through the park when she spied some pretty flowers growing by a clump of trees. She knew her mother loved flowers so she thought about picking some of these for her.

Would Good Citizen Goose pick the flowers for her mother or would she leave them in the park for everyone to enjoy?

At the Playground

Good Citizen Goose and her friends were playing on the swings, when out of the corner of her eye Good Citizen Goose noticed something shiny in the grass. When she went over to look, she discovered that it was a big piece of broken glass.

Would Good Citizen Goose pick up the broken glass and throw it away or leave it alone and report it to an adult?

At the Crosswalk

Good Citizen Goose knows that it is important to be on time. One day she was running late for school. When she got to the intersection where she had to cross the street, she heard a siren. Just then the light turned green and the walk signal came on.

Would Good Citizen Goose stop and wait for the ambulance to pass or would she run across the street so she wouldn't be late?

Shopping

Good Citizen Goose went shopping with her aunt. Just as they were leaving the store, Good Citizen Goose noticed the woman just ahead of them was in a wheelchair and having trouble getting the door open.

Would Good Citizen Goose walk ahead and open the door for the woman or would she just wait patiently until the way was clear?

Books for Parents and Teachers

Educating for Character: How Our Schools Can Teach Respect and Responsibility
by Thomas Lickona (Bantam, 1991)

Although this book is targeted mainly to educators, it contains a wealth of useful information for anyone involved in day-to-day interaction with children.

Bringing Up a Moral Child: Teaching Your Child to be Kind, Just, and Responsible
by Michael Schulman and Eva Mekler (Doubleday, 1985)

An excellent resource and guide for parents and teachers alike, this book offers more than just theory. Through a problem-solving approach, it also provides practical tips for dealing with real-life situations involving children at various age levels.

Books to Read or Share — Trustworthiness

The Boy Who Cried Wolf retold by Katherine Evans (Albert Whitman, 1960)

This is just one version of the classic tale that delivers a powerful message about the importance of being trustworthy and truthful.

Liar, Liar, Pants on Fire by Miriam Cohen (Greenwillow, 1985)

Here is a book that is a perfect springboard for a discussion on truth and honesty. First-grader Alex tells unbelievable stories to get others to notice him.

Just Like Abraham Lincoln by Bernard Waber (Scholastic, 1964)

Mr. Potts looks just like trustworthy Abe Lincoln. He even likes to tell stories about Lincoln to the neighborhood children.

Respect

Bein' With You This Way by W. Nikola-Lisa (Lee & Low, 1994)

Heartfelt illustrations complement a text that has young children discovering that their physical differences only add to the joy of playing and being together.

Oliver Button Is a Sissy by Tomie dePaola (Harcourt Brace Jovanovich, 1979)

Oliver likes to dance, read, and draw pictures rather than play football. His classmates tease him, but eventually come to respect Oliver's uniqueness.

Angel Child, Dragon Child by Michele Maria Surat (Raintree, 1983)

Ut, a Vietnamese child, comes to the United States by herself. Her adjustment is challenging, but made worse by insensitive classmates.

Responsibility

The Little Red Hen by Paul Galdone (Clarion, 1973)

This popular folktale illustrates a lesson in the rewards of hard work and responsibility. The Little Red Hen can't get any of the other animals to help her with the work, but when it is done, they all want to share the rewards.

Arthur Babysits by Marc Brown (Little, Brown, 1992)

Arthur takes on the responsibility of babysitting a pair of twins that are out of control. He tames the terrible twosome by coming up with stories to tell them.

The Salamander Room by Anne Mazer (Albert A. Knopf, 1991)

A young boy finds a beautiful orange salamander and wants to keep it. When it becomes obvious that the salamander has many needs, the boy realizes that it is more responsible to return the animal to its woodland home.

Tidy Titch by Pat Hutchins (Greenwillow, 1991)

This story is about one of the first responsibilities children learn—to clean their rooms.

The Story About Ping by Marjorie Flack and Kurt Wiese (Puffin, 1977)

A little duck learns a difficult lesson about responsibility when he is too late in boarding his master's houseboat one evening.

Fairness

Alexander Who Used to Be Rich Last Sunday by Judith Viorst (Atheneum, 1978)

Alexander thinks it's unfair that his brothers have more money than he does, but he spent his.

Me First by Helen Lester (Houghton Mifflin, 1992)

Greedy Pinkerton Pig always has to be first at everything. He learns a lesson when he rushes to be the first to get a sandwich and finds himself in trouble.

Andy: That's My Name by Tomie dePaola (Prentice Hall, 1973)

This story is a message about fairness (and a fun spelling lesson).

Mike Mulligan and His Steam Shovel by Virginia Lee Burton (Houghton Mifflin, 1939)

In this timeless tale, a smug village official tries to get out of paying Mike and his machine a fair wage.

School Isn't Fair! by Patricia Baehr (Four Winds Press, 1989)

Little Edward describes all the unfair things that happen to him at school.

Caring

Koko's Kitten by Dr. Francine Patterson (Scholastic, 1985)

This is the touching story of a real-life gorilla named Koko who learned sign language. When Koko receives a kitten as a gift, she tenderly loves and cares for it.

Frog and Toad Are Friends by Arnold Lobel (HarperCollins, 1970)

Tales of two special friends who go to great lengths to show they care.

Anna's Secret Friend by Yoriko Tsutsui (Viking Kestrel, 1987)

Anna is excited to move to a new town, but she soon misses her old friends. Her sadness turns to surprise when a secret friend delivers little presents to her.

A New Coat for Anna by Harriet Zeifert (Alfred A. Knopf, 1986)

There is no money to buy Anna a new coat. Although it takes many months, her mother's loving determination produces a beautiful gift.

It's Mine! by Leo Lionni (Alfred A. Knopf, 1985)

Three selfish, frisky frogs fight over everything in their pond home. When a big storm blows in, a toad helps the frogs find the value in kindness and sharing.

The Rainbow Fish by Marcus Pfister (North-South books, 1992)

Children are sure to enjoy this eye-dazzling tale of a beautiful but vain fish who discovers that caring and sharing leads to friendship.

Citizenship

The Gnats of Knotty Pine by Bill Peet (Houghton Mifflin, 1984)

This story illustrates how community members can work together for a common cause. The animals of the woods meet and take action against hunters. The smallest creatures, the gnats, create the plan that foils the hunters.

Old Henry by Joan W. Blos (William Morrow & Company, 1987)

Henry's neighbors don't like the way he keeps his yard, so they run him out of the neighborhood. They then discover that no one is happy after he goes.

The Helping Hands Handbook: A Guidebook for Kids Who Want to Help People, Animals, and the World We Live In by Patricia Adams and Jean Marzollo (Random House, 1992)

Here are over 100 projects kids can do to keep their community safe, clean, enjoyable, and beautiful.

Dear Parents,

Today more than ever our students need to learn more than the three R's to become productive citizens of the future. We hope you will join us in our efforts to strengthen individuals, families, and communities through character education. By instilling in children a strong sense of values we are better preparing them for success as adults.

As parents, you are your children's most important teacher. We encourage you to take advantage of the many opportunities you have at home to reinforce character education. Here are some ideas to consider:

- Children learn by what they see and hear. Be aware of what you are modeling.
- Talk about trust. Be realistic, but avoid creating fearfulness of others.
- Make your expectations clear. Expect honesty and truthfulness, and demonstrate those qualities yourself. Then let your children know that you trust them.
- Keep in mind that respect is more than obedience to authority. True respect is a willful concern for the rights of others and a desire to protect and preserve the value of all things—living and nonliving.
- Share stories and literature that teach lessons. For example, Grimm's fairy tale "The Frog Prince" teaches the value of keeping one's word. "The Little Red Hen" shows how sharing responsibility allows everyone to enjoy the benefits.
- Go out of your way to make sure your child feels that he or she is an important part of the family, especially if your child is the "baby." Explain that everyone in the family has jobs to do and is expected to "pitch in."
- Do not expect a child to take a responsibility that he or she has not been given. But, once you have made your expectations clear, do not accept excuses or do the job for the child.
- Make it a family habit to compliment one another.
- Talk with your child about your "house rules." Explain why each rule is needed—for example, to protect the rights of the family members and to keep them from harm.
- When you must correct a child, be sure to make it clear that it is the *behavior* you disapprove of, not the child. *Example: I know that you are a fair person. That is why it makes me sad to hear that you took more than your share of the clay.*

Thank you for your support!